PLUNGE

Play One of the trilogy
The Ballad of Bimini Baths

Tom Jacobson

BROADWAY PLAY PUBLISHING INC
New York
www.broadwayplaypub.com
info@broadwayplaypub.com

PLUNGE

Cover photo by Matthew McCray

First edition: August 2018
I S B N: 978-0-88145-790-2

Book design: Marie Donovan
Page make-up: Adobe InDesign
Typeface: Palatino

PLUNGE was first produced by Son of Semele Ensemble, opening 26 May 2018. The cast and creative contributors were:

FATHER EDWARD REYNOLDS	Dan Via
EVERETT MAXWELL	Gary Patent
Director	Matt McCray
Scenic design	Michael Fitzgerald
Lighting design	Alexander Le Valliant Freer
Costume design	Michael Mullen
Sound design	David B Marling
Czech translations	Michelle Hanzelova
Spanish translations	Edgar Landa
Stage manager	Daphne Kinard

CHARACTERS & SETTING

REYNOLDS, *40s, a priest, also plays:*
NATRICK, *an attendant*
WILLIAM BOWEN, *an attorney*
ENERNOCIO REMEDIOS, *60s, a laborer*
SANTOS, *an attendant*
YASUNARI, *an attendant*
ZENOBIO REMEDIOS, *13*
FRANK MOODY, *30s, a traveling salesman, English*

MAXWELL, *30s, a curator, also plays:*
YOUNG MAXWELL, *12*
VICTOR LAMAR, *13, Bohemian*
VACLAV LAMAR, *30s, Bohemian*
ZENOBIO REMEDIOS, *13*

The play takes place in a courtyard garden, a prison cell, and various rooms inside Bimini Hot Springs and Sanitorium in 1915-18.

The set should be defined primarily by lighting and words, with a sense of expansiveness at the outset and constriction by the end.

SPECIAL THANKS

Joy Meads, Patricia Garza, Pier Carlo Talenti, Center Theatre Group's L A Writers' Workshop, Son of Semele Ensemble, Lois Arkin, L A Eco Village, Betty Uyeda, John Cahoon, Brent Riggs, Dr William Estrada, Seaver Center for Western History Research, Stan Yogi, Cathy McNassor, Kibo Desoto Knight

SPECIAL THANKS

[illegible]

*(*REYNOLDS*, 40s, handsome, dressed as a priest, sits reading an elegant, leather-bound notebook, equally elegant fountain pen in hand. A champagne glass sits next to him.)*

(Sound of crickets)

REYNOLDS: *(Oklahoma accent, reading)* To the lover of paintings there is nothing to match in interest the human face and form. Rodin once said: "The true artist loves life and action, and he is ever looking for it in his fellow man. The Greeks taught us, both in their marbles and in their drama, that even struggle can be beautiful." *(Smiles, reads)* His face was streaked with sun and shadow, his comely form caressed by a light breeze that bore the tang of the sea. Or perhaps the scent was his honest sweat, hard-earned on our hike up the trail. He saw me smile and turned modestly away, pretending to examine a western tiger swallowtail pausing on a stem of California brome. I reassured him that none could see. *(Corrects with the pen)* I reassured him with a touch that none could see; we were alone. He smiled, his face so open, his eyes so kind. I could see his soul. *(Corrects with the pen)* I could see that the struggle would be beautiful.

*(*MAXWELL*, 30s, appears wearing a tuxedo and carrying a glass of champagne. An open, innocent face. He is searching for something.)*

*(*REYNOLDS *hides the notebook and pen.)*

REYNOLDS: Lost something?

MAXWELL: *(Startled)* Pardon me! I didn't realize—the General's ordered everyone inside—

REYNOLDS: If he's marshalled the troops, you're violating a direct order.

MAXWELL: So are you.

REYNOLDS: Want me to fetch a light?

MAXWELL: Oh, no thank you. It's just—a trifle—

REYNOLDS: I've got sharp eyes.

MAXWELL: No matter. Truly. We should go in or we'll miss remarks.

REYNOLDS: After you.

(Neither MAXWELL *nor* REYNOLDS *moves.)*

MAXWELL: Have we met, Father? I thought the General was—

REYNOLDS: Perhaps we have.	MAXWELL: —Presbyterian —or are you Episcopalian—?

REYNOLDS: Roman Catholic.

MAXWELL: Have you any affiliation with the *Los Angeles Times*? Or society?

REYNOLDS: Good God. You're a snob.

MAXWELL: You're a bit blasphemous for a priest.

REYNOLDS: I'm from Chandler, Oklahoma, where even the clergy are heathen. *(Offers his hand)* Edward Reynolds.

MAXWELL: *(Shaking)* What brings you to the Bivouac, Father Reynolds? Friend of the Otis family?

REYNOLDS: Who?

MAXWELL: General Otis. Harrison Gray Otis. *(Gestures)* The Bivouac—is his house—this is his affair—

REYNOLDS: A bit grand for a bivouac.

MAXWELL: *(Imitating the General)* The Times building is my Fortress, this house is but my Bivouac—

REYNOLDS: You've a talent for mimicry—

MAXWELL: *(Imitating)* —A quaint variation on Mission Revival—with a view of Westlake Park—

REYNOLDS: I thought the *L A Times* was blown up by unionists—

MAXWELL: In fact, this—pavilion— *(Gestures up)* —Is constructed from the rubble of the original Fortress after the bombing—

REYNOLDS: *(Gazing up)* A folly. Isn't that what they're called? Follies. Not pavilions.

MAXWELL: So you can imagine the General is very concerned about security—

MAXWELL: Architectural follies, yes. *(Starts to leave)*

Excuse me—I have charge of the entertainment—

REYNOLDS: Those silly *tableaux vivantes*?

MAXWELL: They depict significant works of art! Perhaps I should introduce myself, Father Reynolds—

REYNOLDS: You're Everett Carroll Maxwell, curator of art at the Los Angeles County Museum of History, Science and Art.

*(*MAXWELL *hesitates.)*

REYNOLDS: And your letter to the editor inspired General Otis to donate his— *(Gestures)* —Bivouac and folly to the Museum as an art school to be named Otis Art Institute.

MAXWELL: You give me too much credit.

REYNOLDS: I'm here tonight to witness your triumph.

MAXWELL: The power of the written word—I suppose—

REYNOLDS: *(Imitating* MAXWELL*)* Nothing exists until written, nothing remembered unless rendered as words. What is not written, is lost.

MAXWELL: You've a talent for mimicry as well. It's flattering but unnerving to be quoted by a complete stranger. Good evening, Father.

*(*MAXWELL *starts to leave.* REYNOLDS *suddenly takes the pose of The Thinker.)*

REYNOLDS: Picture me nude.

MAXWELL: I've never heard a priest speak like that!

REYNOLDS: Neither has my congregation. You're not my congregation. Are you?

MAXWELL: You'll have to try harder than that. *The Poet.*

REYNOLDS: *The Thinker*—by Rodin!

MAXWELL: Originally called *Le Poete*. The foundry workers dubbed it *The Thinker* because it resembled Michelangelo's statue *Il Penseroso.* Too easy.

REYNOLDS: Then let's try one together.

MAXWELL: Oh, no.

REYNOLDS: Heracles wrestling Antaeus.

MAXWELL: You know your Greek.

MAXWELL: Whose version?

REYNOLDS: Antaeus could defeat his opponents—

REYNOLDS: —As long as he was touching his mother, the earth. Heracles beat him—

MAXWELL: —By lifting him in the air and crushing him—

REYNOLDS: —By hoisting him aloft before bringing him low—

MAXWELL: —Yes, of course, but which artist's rendition? Antonio del Pollaiulo?

REYNOLDS: Vincenzo di Rossi.

MAXWELL: You know too much art history for your own good!

REYNOLDS: The dyametrical opposition of the bodies in a vertical orientation—

MAXWELL: Like the figure 69—

REYNOLDS: —With Antaeus gripping Heracles by the gonads—

MAXWELL: It's vulgar—the least artistic representation—

REYNOLDS: But the most dramatic.

REYNOLDS: *(Advancing on* MAXWELL*)* Shall we attempt it—?

MAXWELL: No, someone might see—!

REYNOLDS: *(Grabbing* MAXWELL*)* We're answering an artistic question—

REYNOLDS: —Determining which is superior—

MAXWELL: Who's Hercules and who's Antaeus?!

REYNOLDS: *(Easily lifting* MAXWELL*)* That depends on who wins!

MAXWELL: *(Struggling)* This a society affair!

*(*REYNOLDS *turns* MAXWELL *upside down.)*

MAXWELL: Father Reynolds! Put me down!

*(*MAXWELL *wriggles free and falls. The notebook falls to the ground as well.* REYNOLDS *moves to help him up.)*

REYNOLDS: Mr Maxwell, my apologies—let me—!

MAXWELL: No!

*(*MAXWELL *waves him away and stands on his own, looking around to see if they were observed. They see the notebook on the ground.)*

BOTH: Oh.

REYNOLDS: *(Picks it up)* Sermon notes.

MAXWELL: Ah.

REYNOLDS: *(Pocketing the notebook)* I had assumed you a more athletic sort—

MAXWELL: I'm a journalist!

REYNOLDS: —With your scouting activities, tramping about with children on field trips—

MAXWELL: I lure them to the Museum with tar pit fossils then trick them into enjoying art.

REYNOLDS: You seduce them with old bones?

MAXWELL: Gruesomeness appeals to that age. The dramatic deaths of mastodons trapped in tar thousands of years ago, the fang of a sabertooth, the pelvis of a giant ground sloth—

REYNOLDS: Are you collecting objects or collecting people?

MAXWELL: I beg your pardon?

REYNOLDS: As General Otis has collected you. A prominent art curator and journalist, a rare species.

MAXWELL: You've overestimated my importance to society. My father was a cabinet maker. We had to take in boarders.

REYNOLDS: But art elevated you.

MAXWELL: One of the boarders, actually. Professor Frank Moody introduced me to the glories of the Renaissance.

REYNOLDS: *(Imitating* MAXWELL*)* The purpose of art is empathy.

MAXWELL: Your accuracy borders on cruelty. But I do believe that.

REYNOLDS: And yet you are not yourself an artist.

MAXWELL: Writers are artists!

REYNOLDS: Of analysis! Criticism!

MAXWELL: What I really want to do is write screenplays.

(REYNOLDS *smiles.)*

MAXWELL: Motion pictures are the art form of the future. A *gesamtkunstwerk* of empathy!

REYNOLDS: Is that Bohemian?

MAXWELL: No, German. I'm friends with a Bohemian artist—

REYNOLDS: Max Wieczorek.

MAXWELL: *(Suspiciously)* Yes…why do you ask?

REYNOLDS: Chandler is right next to Prague, Oklahoma—full of Bohunks. I'm visiting the Lamar family here in Los Angeles—

MAXWELL: Lamar?

REYNOLDS: —Relatives of parishoners in Oklahoma—

MAXWELL: I've heard that name—

REYNOLDS: *(Takes out the notebook)* And I should get back. An honor to meet such a pillar of society— *(Starts to go)*

MAXWELL: Father—

REYNOLDS: I must catch my streetcar—

MAXWELL: Why did you become a priest?

REYNOLDS: That's an odd and personal question. And what of your remarks?

MAXWELL: They can wait a moment, I'm sure. How often does one have a chance to speak privately with clergy?

REYNOLDS: Have you a particular need for a priest this evening? A moral question?

MAXWELL: Yours is a profession steeped in sacrifice.

REYNOLDS: Which you well understand. Your devotion to your invalid mother—your father—

MAXWELL: They're my parents—I'm an only child—of course—

MAXWELL: —But how do you know—?	REYNOLDS: Filial constancy.

MAXWELL: You have me at great disadvantage—I know nothing about you!

REYNOLDS: You're famous.

MAXWELL: What called you to the priesthood?

REYNOLDS: Other than God?

MAXWELL: I was inculcated in art. Had you similar tutelage?

REYNOLDS: A priestly temperament is not always the same as an artistic one.

MAXWELL: But sometimes.

REYNOLDS: I was drawn to the intelligence and serenity of the Dominicans. Nothing prissy or picayune about their faith. A way out of annihilation.

MAXWELL: Annihilation!?

REYNOLDS: The priesthood showed me how someone worthless could throw himself away without literally killing himself.

MAXWELL: That's a breath-takingly cynical way of saying the church saved you in your *noche oscura de alma.*

REYNOLDS: As art saved you in your dark night of the soul.

MAXWELL: Did you truly consider suicide?

REYNOLDS: *(Shrugs)* Christ did that for us.

MAXWELL: Whenever I see a crucifixion—a good crucifixion—I feel his suffering so keenly I'm moved to tears.

REYNOLDS: Do you desire punishment?

MAXWELL: That's what priests offer! Judgment! Doom!

REYNOLDS: Is that what you seek?

MAXWELL: You're the one seeking annihiliation.

REYNOLDS: Salvation is what I hope I offer. Confession. Absolution. Christ's suffering not punishment but atonement.

*(*MAXWELL *takes a twisted pose, his hands above his head, his gaze heavenward.)*

REYNOLDS: Some martyr, but they all look alike to me. Are you male or female?

MAXWELL: It's Oscar Wilde's favorite painting.

REYNOLDS: Male, then.

MAXWELL: Picture me pierced with arrows!

REYNOLDS: Saint Sebastian.

MAXWELL: *(Relaxing)* Guido Reni's *Saint Sebastian*. Even in agony, his eyes are so kind.

REYNOLDS: As are yours.

*(*MAXWELL *and* REYNOLDS *smile.)*

MAXWELL: Please let me help you, Father.

REYNOLDS: May I ask you something?

MAXWELL: Of course, Father.

REYNOLDS: It's confidential.

MAXWELL: Does it have to do with your sermon notes?

REYNOLDS: Possibly. I may be going mad.

MAXWELL: Mad? You seem perfectly—

REYNOLDS: I won't give you details here, but I've suffered a number of symptoms—hallucinations—

MAXWELL: Hallucinations?

REYNOLDS: People who aren't really there—I'm sorry—

REYNOLDS: —Someone might hear—	MAXWELL: Let me assure you I'm truly here.

MAXWELL: A private conversation, of course! Where are you staying in Los Angeles?

REYNOLDS: On Centennial Street. But we can't go there. And you live with your parents.

MAXWELL: How long have you been visiting?

REYNOLDS: Just arrived today.

MAXWELL: So you haven't been to Bimini Baths?

REYNOLDS: What's that?

MAXWELL: A natural hot spring resort and sanitarium at the edge of town.

REYNOLDS: Nearby?

MAXWELL: On Vermont. Fifteen minutes by streetcar, the Heliotrope Line.

REYNOLDS: A public bathing facility?

MAXWELL: There are private tub baths as well.

REYNOLDS: I am rather desperate for a thorough cleansing after my journey.

MAXWELL: They are renowned for their purges.

REYNOLDS: What of your remarks?

MAXWELL: Your need sounds urgent and I wish to be of service—

REYNOLDS: My suffering should in no way diminish your social victory this evening.

MAXWELL: Of course, but immediately—

REYNOLDS: *(Overlapping)* Immediately after.

(Lighting shift isolates REYNOLDS *as* MAXWELL *begins his remarks.)*

MAXWELL: Ladies and gentlemen of Los Angeles. Our fair western city has grown by leaps and bounds in the seventeen years since the century turned.

(As MAXWELL *speaks,* REYNOLDS *begins undressing.)*

MAXWELL: Not only in size, but also in maturity, sophistication. Only four years ago we stepped into the cultural arena with the founding of the Los Angeles County Museum of History, Science and Art.

*(*MAXWELL *can see* REYNOLDS *stripping down, revealing an early 20th-century bathing costume.)*

MAXWELL: Tonight, thanks to the foresight of our host, General Harrison Gray Otis, we embark upon a new journey with the donation of the Bivouac to the people of Los Angeles for the advancement of art in the West.

*(*REYNOLDS'*s change of costume distracts* MAXWELL, *but he holds himself together to finish his speech.)*

MAXWELL: His aims for the new Otis Art Institute are broad and comprehensive, and include the fostering of the Fine, the Applied and the Industrial Arts. *(Slightly agitated)* No one person in Southern California has yet made so important a contribution to the cause of art education in the great Southwest. So I invite you to raise a glass to my friend General Otis— *(Raises glass)* —And to art!

(Lighting shift puts REYNOLDS *and* MAXWELL *in the same space.)*

*(*REYNOLDS *is looking at a brochure.)*

MAXWELL: What is it you wished to tell me, Father? You sounded so urgent—

REYNOLDS: The swimming plunges are open until 10 P M.

MAXWELL: *(Overlapping)* Ten P M, yes, I know, but—

REYNOLDS: Do you have a bathing costume?

MAXWELL: *(Begins changing)* Of course. I'm here with some frequency.

REYNOLDS: *(Reading)* "Bimini Baths was named for Ponce de Leon's mythical Fountain of Youth. The famous hot spring was struck in 1900 when boring for oil. At a depth of one thousand seven hundred and fifty feet the drill passed through a hard crust of soda—which at the time was mistaken for white marble—and opened a gushing fountain of mineral water with a natural and constant flow of a hundred gallons per minute at a hundred and four degrees Fahrenheit. This water, flowing as it does through petroleum strata, is impregnated, not with petroleum gas and petroleum in emulsion, but also carries some of the medicinal properties which are derived form cure petroleum and which are not used in their various forms by our leading physicians." Shall we start with the plunge?

MAXWELL: For proper cleansing, we should end with the plunge after a treatment or two.

REYNOLDS: *(Looking off)* Is Bimini Baths exclusive?

MAXWELL: It's very popular with Los Angeles society. You might even spy a motion picture star. They come to Hollywood seeking the Fountain of Youth.

REYNOLDS: Isn't the undesirable element prohibited?

MAXWELL: *(Looking around)* Undesirable? Where?

REYNOLDS: That man is black.

MAXWELL: What man? I don't see—

REYNOLDS: In the white jacket.

MAXWELL: Perhaps he's an employee, an attendant.

REYNOLDS: I wouldn't want to bathe in the same water—

MAXWELL: The jacket is a uniform.

REYNOLDS: We don't have such fancy resorts in Oklahoma, but we do maintain proper segregation of the races—

MAXWELL: Bimini's exclusive, I'm quite certain—

(When MAXWELL *turns away,* REYNOLDS *dons a white jacket and becomes* NATRICK.*)*

MAXWELL: —You needn't be anxious—

REYNOLDS AS NATRICK: *(Jamaican accent)* Good evening, gentlemen. Welcome to the Hydrotherapy Department.

MAXWELL: *(Staring, confused)* What?

REYNOLDS AS NATRICK: My apologies, Mr Maxwell. I didn't mean to startle you.

MAXWELL: I'm sorry—I—

REYNOLDS AS NATRICK: And I hope I'm not interrupting—

MAXWELL: No, not at all!

REYNOLDS AS NATRICK: I understand you've purchased a full course of treatments.

MAXWELL: Yes, we have, but—

REYNOLDS AS NATRICK: The management recommends commencing with the Hot Pelvic Pack followed by a purge such as a high enema.

MAXWELL: What—what is your name?

REYNOLDS AS NATRICK: Natrick, sir.

MAXWELL: Patrick?

REYNOLDS AS NATRICK: Begging your pardon, sir—it's Natrick.

MAXWELL: Natrick. Thank you. Could you tell us about the other treatments on our menu? My companion seeks satisfaction regarding the cleanliness of your facility and sulfur water.

REYNOLDS AS NATRICK: *(Applying a pelvic pack)* Certainly, sir. The hot pelvic pack is infused with naturally heated Bimini water, not sulfur water as many mistakenly believe, but a thermal solution containing sodium carbonate, sodium chloride, potassium chloride, silica, calcium carbonate, magnesium carbonate, iron and aluminum.

(While MAXWELL *adjusts his pelvic pack,* REYNOLDS *removes the jacket.)*

MAXWELL: A perfect initiation of the cleansing process.

REYNOLDS: Are all those chemicals safe?

*(*MAXWELL *reacts to* NATRICK *turning back into* REYNOLDS.*)*

MAXWELL: Oh! My! Did you—?

*(*MAXWELL *looks around for* NATRICK.*)*

REYNOLDS: Do you think the water is safe with all those…ingredients?

MAXWELL: *(Stifling his confusion)* Of course, Father, it's not only hygienic, but also nearly identical to the spa waters of Europe, known for their curative properties.

REYNOLDS: *(Looking to make sure* NATRICK *is gone)*

They should have white attendants. We paid good money.

MAXWELL: This pelvic pack is hot!

REYNOLDS: What's it supposed to do?

MAXWELL: I imagine it's both therapeutic and relaxing.

REYNOLDS: It has a bit of an odor.

MAXWELL & REYNOLDS: But not sulfur! *(They laugh)*

MAXWELL: Father, back at the Bivouac you seemed distressed and asked for a private word. Did you wish to speak to me of…annihilation?

REYNOLDS: We are in bathing attire. You may call me Edward.

MAXWELL: And please call me Everett. Only my students call me Mr Maxwell.

REYNOLDS: With pleasure, Everett.

MAXWELL: You mentioned feeling worthless. Is it—all right to—Edward—?

REYNOLDS: These rooms are truly private?

MAXWELL: Until Mr Natrick returns.

REYNOLDS: As you intuited, the church did indeed save me, provide a refuge. But there are still times I feel myself a negative force in the world—

MAXWELL: You're a priest! God's representative—

REYNOLDS: Nevertheless, I wonder if it might be better for everyone else if I were…not here.

MAXWELL: Dead? Surely not!

REYNOLDS: Priests are not perfect.

MAXWELL: You are human.

REYNOLDS: Have you heard of sexual inversion?

MAXWELL: Possibly…if you mean—

REYNOLDS: Alienists regard it either a perversion, a moral failing, or incurable degeneration.

MAXWELL: Have you consulted a psychiatrist, Father? That is, if you feel you might suffer from such a condition?

REYNOLDS: It's why I came to Los Angeles. Alienists are few and far between in Oklahoma, and not in the least progressive.

MAXWELL: You've seen one already? And what has he told you?

REYNOLDS: He subjected me to certain physical examinations and electrode testing.

MAXWELL: Electrodes!

REYNOLDS: Shocks to the anus.

MAXWELL: Was there a…noticeable result?

REYNOLDS: Intense puckering of the sphincter is evidence of the vice.

MAXWELL: The mere description has given me a bit of a pucker.

REYNOLDS: He suggested an exercise. For a measure of relief.

MAXWELL: Sit-ups?

REYNOLDS: For the rectum. Butt-ups, if you will. I'm doing it.

MAXWELL: At this moment?

REYNOLDS: Alternating tension and relaxation.

MAXWELL: I see.

REYNOLDS: Try it.

*(*MAXWELL *and* REYNOLDS *sit quietly doing butt-ups.)*

MAXWELL: *(After a moment)* And this relieves degenerate urges?

REYNOLDS: *(After a moment)* I've just begun treatment, so I've yet to see much result.

MAXWELL: *(After a moment)* In conjunction with the hot pelvic pack, the effect is profound.

REYNOLDS: Yes, it's encouraging.

MAXWELL: Did he tell you anything else?

REYNOLDS: Penile deformities are also indicative. Apparently.

MAXWELL: Deformities? Of what nature, may I ask?

REYNOLDS: It is, as you might imagine, quite embarrassing.

MAXWELL: Yes, of course, and very personal. I apologize!

REYNOLDS: Excessive size.

MAXWELL: That makes sense.

REYNOLDS: It's a burden.

MAXWELL: Did your alienist recommend treatment for that?

REYNOLDS: Strangely, no. His views are evolving as progress is made in the medical and psychiatric fields. By the end of his life Krafft-Ebing regarded inversion as a mental illness but not utter insanity.

MAXWELL: I am happy to know it.

REYNOLDS: Happy? That I'm mentally ill?

MAXWELL: Not insane.

REYNOLDS: Havelock Ellis called it a sport of nature.

MAXWELL: In other words, a variant, not a degeneration.

REYNOLDS: Exactly! At one end of a spectrum, but within the realm of normal.

MAXWELL: Father—

BOTH: Edward—!

MAXWELL: I understand your distress, but surely your psychiatrist has told you there exist many men like yourself.

REYNOLDS: Many?

MAXWELL: I, myself, have encountered more than a few.

REYNOLDS: I thought you might have, being in the arts.

MAXWELL: So I presume he has persuaded you from self-annihilation.

REYNOLDS: That isn't really what I wanted to tell you.

MAXWELL: Oh. I'm sorry. I thought—

REYNOLDS: I've made peace with it, as you've suggested.

MAXWELL: There's some other reason you feel worthless to society?

REYNOLDS: I'm afraid so.

MAXWELL: Worse than inversion?

REYNOLDS: I don't wish to disturb you—

MAXWELL: No, no, I'm flattered to be trusted upon so short an acquaintance.

REYNOLDS: I had hoped you'd understand.

MAXWELL: Indeed! I am…a very understanding person.

REYNOLDS: Empathic. As when you view a crucifixion.

MAXWELL: I like to think so.

REYNOLDS: Critical to your art training.

MAXWELL: Your training as a priest must have been similarly beneficial. The church is founded on compassion. Surely you feel welcome there.

REYNOLDS: That's part of the problem.

MAXWELL: Too much compassion?

REYNOLDS: It's a sanctuary. For men like myself.

MAXWELL: So you are...not alone. Are you concerned about...overstimulation?

REYNOLDS: Not in Chandler, Oklahoma.

MAXWELL: Of course.

REYNOLDS: But the church provides a certain structure, situations—I will even go so far as to say the word "protections—"

MAXWELL: Which I imagine is helpful to you.

REYNOLDS: In an unhelpful way.

MAXWELL: I'm afraid you're exceeding my capacity to comprehend.

REYNOLDS: Your volunteer work in the community includes activities with the Boy Scouts.

MAXWELL: Yes, the South Pasadena troop. Why?

REYNOLDS: There are no men like myself in Chandler. But among my duties as priest is religious instruction of youth.

MAXWELL: Ah.

REYNOLDS: At that age, there are many questions, only a few related to the Old and New Testaments.

MAXWELL: I'm sure you provide proper guidance.

REYNOLDS: Some youths seek understanding, are psychologically vulnerable—

MAXWELL: It's your calling to listen—

REYNOLDS: To remind them they're God's children—

MAXWELL: And special—

REYNOLDS: Yes, to make them feel—

MAXWELL: You give them something no one else can.

REYNOLDS: Who better to teach them than I?

MAXWELL: God's representative—compassionate—

REYNOLDS: Gentle.

MAXWELL: Kind.

REYNOLDS: I'm helping them.

MAXWELL: Yes, only helping.

REYNOLDS: You understand.

MAXWELL: I—I—

REYNOLDS: This is not always understood.

(MAXWELL *is quiet.)*

REYNOLDS: I apologize. I never should have—

MAXWELL: No, no. Ordinarily I would find it impossible to sympathize with such a person, someone suffering from this form of illness—if I may use that word as it's another thing entirely from—inversion—much more to my mind a question of sanity—

REYNOLDS: Do you consider what I've done with those boys a capital crime?

MAXWELL: Deserving death? No, if that's why you—

REYNOLDS: I'm sorry I told you—

MAXWELL: But even though I could never understand, never enter the mind of such a one, you seem to me utterly—normal—in every respect, not dissimilar from myself—

REYNOLDS: We'll say no more about it.

MAXWELL: You had to leave Oklahoma?

REYNOLDS: The Bishop suggested I…explore the West while he assigns me another parish.

MAXWELL: How very thoughtful of him.

REYNOLDS: Is it?

MAXWELL: He understands.

REYNOLDS: He takes my confession.

MAXWELL: As I am now.

REYNOLDS: You see this as confession?

MAXWELL: Isn't that how it's offered? Even with the bishop's understanding, it preys on you.

REYNOLDS: It isn't right, is it? My only punishment reassignment.

MAXWELL: Do you desire punishment?

REYNOLDS: I'm Catholic.

MAXWELL: Did you hurt anyone?

REYNOLDS: No! Not physically, I mean.

MAXWELL: And you're repentant.

REYNOLDS: The parents don't feel two Hail Marys and an Our Father are quite enough.

MAXWELL: Your entire life is uprooted! Everything you built at your parish in Oklahoma gone! That is certainly atonement. And you'll not do it again. *(Silence)* Will you?

REYNOLDS: Perhaps only sin can erase sin.

MAXWELL: Suicide is mortal sin.

REYNOLDS: As mortal as it gets.

MAXWELL: Which is why you seek my counsel?

REYNOLDS: It's not often someone understands. *(Proffers the notebook)*

MAXWELL: I've just told you I do not understand.

REYNOLDS: But you've listened.

MAXWELL: You wish to share your sermon notes?

(REYNOLDS *only smiles)*

MAXWELL: This kind of writing is highly personal. I'd be embarrassed to read it.

(REYNOLDS *doesn't move.)*

MAXWELL: Very well, I will take it if you insist. *(Takes the notebook)* But I won't look at it in front of you— *(Starts to pocket it)*

REYNOLDS: Don't you want to help me?

MAXWELL: I'd prefer to know your intimate thoughts in private, at home, if you really wish me to. We can talk about them another day.

REYNOLDS: I can't let that notebook out of my sight.

MAXWELL: Why not?

REYNOLDS: It contains my soul. *(Reaches for it)* Never mind—I won't burden you—

MAXWELL: *(Snatching the notebook back)* You've made it my moral duty. If this is your immortal soul.

REYNOLDS: Thank you.

MAXWELL: *(Flipping through the notebook)* Shall I—from the beginning—?

REYNOLDS: Only this last section— *(Points)* —Starting with "December 6, 1915—"

MAXWELL: *(After a moment)* On December 6, 1915, I led a group of lads on a hike through the tall grass of the Arroyo Seco: Ben Covert (age 17)—

REYNOLDS: Huh.

MAXWELL: Clifford Stanley (age 16), his brother Frederick Stanley (age 18), and Zenobio Remedios (age 16)—

REYNOLDS: Fifteen.

MAXWELL: What?

REYNOLDS: It's fifteen, not sixteen.

MAXWELL: It says sixteen.

REYNOLDS: It should say fifteen. *(Hands him the pen)* Could you correct it, please?

MAXWELL: It's your notes.

REYNOLDS: Nothing exists until written.

MAXWELL: *(Makes the change)* And Zenobio Remedios (age 15). At the end of our walk, the boys grew boisterous while waiting for their parents. There was much ribaldry over a pair of turtles we surprised during mating. The male fell on his back while still attached to the female, and she proceeded to run away—as fast as a tortoise can run—dragging him behind her, his stubby limbs flailing. I persuaded the boys to leave the amorous pair to their privacy. One by one, the youngsters departed with their parents, until only Zeno remained. A bright boy, fluent in both English and Spanish— *(To* REYNOLDS*)* You speak Spanish?

REYNOLDS: *No hablo.*

MAXWELL: Then how do you know he's fluent?

REYNOLDS: Overheard him with his *abuelo.*

MAXWELL: Fluent in both English and Spanish, Zeno is fascinated—

REYNOLDS: *(After a moment)* What fascinates him?

MAXWELL: Zeno is fascinated with the remains of dire wolves from the La Brea Tar Pits. He wants to study paleontology at Yale and was delighted some weeks ago when I gave him a wolf baculum from the Museum's excavations—

REYNOLDS: You know what a baculum is?

MAXWELL: A penis bone. *(To* REYNOLDS*)* How much more—?

REYNOLDS: A bit.

MAXWELL: We waited together for Zeno's *abuelo.* His face was streaked with sun and shadow, his comely form caressed by a light breeze that bore the tang of the sea. Or perhaps the scent was his honest sweat, hard-earned on our hike up the trail. He saw me smile and turned modestly away, pretending to examine a western tiger swallowtail pausing on a stem of California brome. I reassured him with a touch that none could see—

REYNOLDS: Keep going.

MAXWELL: This—this isn't—

REYNOLDS: Isn't what?

MAXWELL: Nothing. *(Resumes reading)* We were alone. He smiled, his face so open, his eyes so kind. I could see—

REYNOLDS: What?

MAXWELL: It's not—correct—

REYNOLDS: How would you know?

MAXWELL: Don't mock me.

REYNOLDS: Read it.

MAXWELL: It's false!

REYNOLDS: Why would a lie in my sermon notes matter to you? Keep reading.

MAXWELL: *(With great effort)* I could see that—I can't—

REYNOLDS: I could see that the struggle—

MAXWELL: I won't!

REYNOLDS: I could see that the struggle would be beautiful.

MAXWELL: It's been altered.

REYNOLDS: Check the handwriting.

MAXWELL: That's not what I wrote!

REYNOLDS: Your name is on it.

MAXWELL: Pickpocket!

REYNOLDS: You should keep better track of your words. In the wrong hands, that notebook will destroy you.

MAXWELL: Your hands!

REYNOLDS: Your hands. I've given it back as proof you can trust me. You needn't fear me. I'm you.

MAXWELL: Everyone who knows me agrees the charges are fabricated—

REYNOLDS: The Museum's taking your side—

MAXWELL: Of course! President Bowen said—

REYNOLDS: *(Becoming* BOWEN, *pompous)* The charge against Mr Maxwell is absurd. I have known him for more than five years and he is a man of the highest character.

MAXWELL: Yes!

REYNOLDS AS BOWEN: If this case ever comes to trial— He has thousands of friends in art and literary circles of Southern California—

MAXWELL: That's true! Thousands!	REYNOLDS AS BOWEN: —Who will testify to his high qualities.

REYNOLDS AS BOWEN: In my mind this difficulty is a case of mistaken identity.

MAXWELL: That's very possible. But how did you—?

REYNOLDS: *(Becoming himself)* Mistaken identity, truly?

MAXWELL: Or it's a conspiracy—the parents—

REYNOLDS: The parents know each other?

MAXWELL: From the Y M C A, the South Pasadena Scout troop—Mr and Mrs Stanley, Ben and Edna Covert, Enernocion and Candelario Remedios—

REYNOLDS: Why would they conspire? Why lie?

MAXWELL: I am not that person!

REYNOLDS: You give their boys a gift, teaching them about science, swimming, taking them on nature walks, to the Museum—

MAXWELL: They're jealous!

REYNOLDS: Jealous?

MAXWELL: Envious of the opportunities—

MAXWELL: I get on with the boys better than their parents—they're poor, desperately poor—I know what that's like. You want the best for your children, but when they learn new things, enter a world you can't—my own father resented my art studies—

REYNOLDS: The parents brought charges against you to spite their children?

MAXWELL: The vitriol is shocking. I was completely unprepared.

REYNOLDS: They confronted you directly?

MAXWELL: Officer Johnston brought Enernocion Remedios to my home!

REYNOLDS: The night you were arrested?

MAXWELL: Intimidation, an invasion, an assault—!

REYNOLDS: *(Becomes* ENERNOCIO*)* *¿Qué ha hecho con mi nieto? ¡Monstruo! Lo ha ensuciado! Ha manchado su alma!* [What have you done to my grandson? You monster! You have soiled him! Tainted his very soul!]

MAXWELL: No, Señor Remedio—! *Me preocupo por su niño!* [I care for your boy!]

REYNOLDS AS ENERNOCIO: *Lo atrajo con viajes y placeres, y luego aprovechado su inocencia!* [Lured him with trips and pleasures, then taken advantage of his innocence!]

MAXWELL: *No sé de que habla!* [I don't know what you're talking about!]

REYNOLDS AS ENERNOCIO: *Lo engaño y lo robo de sus queridos padres! ¡Maldito! Diablo blanco!* [Stolen him away from his loving parents with sinful trickery! You are evil! A white devil!]

REYNOLDS AS ENERNOCIO: *Confesarse! Limpieze el alma!* [Confess! Cleanse yourself!]

MAXWELL: I thought you didn't speak Spanish. Mimicry is the opposite of empathy.

REYNOLDS: You've been abused. I see that. By the police, the parents, *un abuelo mojado*—

MAXWELL: I can't fathom his rage. It is beyond me.

REYNOLDS: You didn't hurt anyone.

MAXWELL: And Zeno is a wonderful boy! Smart and curious. As much as I try to steer him to art, he dreams of being a scientist.

*(*REYNOLDS *puts on a white jacket.)*

MAXWELL: Perhaps his grandfather's afraid of that, the expense of college—

*(*REYNOLDS *becomes* SANTOS, *an attendant.)*

REYNOLDS AS SANTOS: *(Mexican accent)* Gentlemen, apologies for interrupting your conversation—

MAXWELL: Oh! Is it—? Who are you?

REYNOLDS AS SANTOS: *Mi nombre es Santos*. I'm on staff.

MAXWELL: *Mucho gusto, Señor Santos.*

REYNOLDS AS SANTOS: *(Slyly) Usted entiende. Oi decir que habla espanol.* [You understand. I heard you speak Spanish.] *(Smiles) Si, entiendo. Entiende usted?* [I understand. Do you understand?]

MAXWELL: *(Shaken)* I understand.

REYNOLDS AS SANTOS: *Bueno.* Are you ready to proceed to the Department of Mechano Therapy?

MAXWELL: I hadn't realized it was time—

REYNOLDS AS SANTOS: Your treatment course provides a number of choices—

REYNOLDS AS SANTOS: Including camphor, hamamelis and methol rubs with salt glow, saline friction with salt rub, and alcohol rub with manipulations. *Pase por aqui, por favor.* [This way, please.]

*(*MAXWELL *goes with* REYNOLDS AS SANTOS.*)*

MAXWELL: Have you Swedish massage?

REYNOLDS AS SANTOS: *Si, Señor.* Are you experiencing tension?

MAXWELL: Yes! A great deal!

REYNOLDS AS SANTOS: Then we recommend Schotts Movements.

MAXWELL: What are those?

REYNOLDS AS SANTOS: Schotts gymnastics consist of passive and active, excentric and concentric movements. *(Manipulates* MAXWELL*'s body)* At first the patient goes through passive manipulation of the phalangeal joints, later the larger joints.

MAXWELL: Have you tried it yourself?

REYNOLDS AS SANTOS: Oh, no, *Señor*, I'm not allowed. Please remove the top portion of your bathing costume.

*(*MAXWELL *does.)*

MAXWELL: And this provides relief?

REYNOLDS AS SANTOS: *Sin duda, Señor.* These movements are performed by the operator synchronously with the patient's respiratory movements. Very slowly.

(MAXWELL *performs the movements while* REYNOLDS *removes the white jacket and the top portion of his bathing costume.)*

MAXWELL: I see. Coordinated with the breathing.

(REYNOLDS *moves in parallel with* MAXWELL.)

REYNOLDS: Young Zeno is a scientist?

MAXWELL: Budding. More curious than skilled, of course.

REYNOLDS: Trusting?

MAXWELL: With every reason to be so!

REYNOLDS: Victor's trusting like that.

MAXWELL: Who?

REYNOLDS: Victor Lamar.

MAXWELL: That name is familiar.

REYNOLDS: The young son of the Bohunk family I'm staying with.

MAXWELL: How old is he?

REYNOLDS: Fifteen.

MAXWELL: Ah.

REYNOLDS: But trusting does not mean trustworthy. I know these boys.

MAXWELL: Zeno is entirely trustworthy!

REYNOLDS: He didn't complain about you to his *abuelo*?

MAXWELL: He's devoted to me!

(REYNOLDS *becomes* ZENO.)

MAXWELL: Working class but extraordinarily polite.

REYNOLDS AS ZENO: *(Spanish accent)* Mr Maxwell, who's the best artist in the world?

MAXWELL: Zeno, what a marvelous question!

REYNOLDS AS ZENO: Is it Picasso?

MAXWELL: Many people think so, but art is more than ideas.

REYNOLDS AS ZENO: It's feelings.

MAXWELL: And whose paintings make you feel?

REYNOLDS AS ZENO: Lots!

MAXWELL: Maybe there's more than one right answer. What artist makes you feel the most?

REYNOLDS AS ZENO: Albert Bierstadt.

MAXWELL: Bierstadt? Why?

REYNOLDS AS ZENO: When I see the beautiful places he paints, I want to go there.

MAXWELL: What about portrait painters?

REYNOLDS AS ZENO: You mean your friend with the funny name?

MAXWELL: It's not funny, it's Bohemian! Max Wieczorek.

REYNOLDS AS ZENO: His name is hard to say, but I like his people. They make me feel…nice.

MAXWELL: Nice? Do you mean passion?

REYNOLDS AS ZENO: What's passion?

MAXWELL: A very strong feeling, overwhelming, out of control.

REYNOLDS AS ZENO: Happy or sad?

MAXWELL: Both.

REYNOLDS AS ZENO: Strange?

MAXWELL: Yes.

REYNOLDS AS ZENO: Can it hurt?

MAXWELL: That, too. Everything all at once.

REYNOLDS AS ZENO: Oh, then I know one!

MAXWELL: Who?

REYNOLDS AS ZENO: I'll show you.

MAXWELL: If you wish.

(REYNOLDS AS ZENO *takes the Guido Reni Saint Sebastian pose.)*

REYNOLDS AS ZENO: Do you get it?

MAXWELL: I'm not sure.

REYNOLDS AS ZENO: Tie my hands!

MAXWELL: With what?

REYNOLDS AS ZENO: *(Motions)* There's a piece of rope.

MAXWELL: I can guess without—

REYNOLDS AS ZENO: Tie me! Then stick me full of arrows!

MAXWELL: Saint Sebastian!

REYNOLDS AS ZENO: By Guido Reni!

MAXWELL: Why do you like that one the best?

REYNOLDS AS ZENO: It makes me feel like Saint Sebastian—sad, happy and strange and hurting all at once. Passion!

MAXWELL: Zeno, you're a very smart lad.

REYNOLDS AS ZENO: Guido Reni is the best artist ever.

MAXWELL: Best for you, my intelligent young friend. You're absolutely right.

(REYNOLDS *changes back to himself, resuming the Schotts movements.)*

REYNOLDS: He asked you to tie him up?

MAXWELL: I didn't! And I knew which painting all along, of course.

REYNOLDS: Of course. Pedophilia is sexual attraction to prepubescent children.

MAXWELL: I'm not a pedophile!

REYNOLDS: That's my point. Neither Zeno nor Victor was under eleven.

MAXWELL: Zeno was fourteen.

REYNOLDS: Fourteen, yes. Hebephilia is what they call it when the young person is in puberty, ages eleven through fourteen. Still a legal issue at that age, in any case.

MAXWELL: You're acting as if I've confessed to the crime. I have not!

REYNOLDS: Almost all adults, and certainly all adult males, are attracted to young people ages sixteen to nineteen.

MAXWELL: That's only normal. They're physiological adults.

REYNOLDS: Ephebophilia, it's called. Magnus Hirschfeld regards it as normal and nonpathological.

MAXWELL: You know rather a lot about it for a priest.

REYNOLDS: What better study than oneself?

(REYNOLDS *dons the white jacket, becoming* YASUNARI.)

MAXWELL: Have you discovered why you are the way you are? Why you have this...preference? Something that happened to you as a child?

REYNOLDS AS YASUNARI: *(Japanese accent)* Mr Maxwell, my name is Yasunari. May I take you to Department of Electro Therapy?

MAXWELL: Actually, Mr Yasunari, we're still—

REYNOLDS AS YASUNARI: Your course of treatments must progress without delay if you're to finish before closing.

MAXWELL: What are our choices in Electro Therapy?

REYNOLDS AS YASUNARI: The electric tub bath, high frequency treatment, thermo therapeutic oven for joints, vibratory treatment—

MAXWELL: *(Going with* REYNOLDS AS YASUNARI*)* Any radio-active treatments?

REYNOLDS AS YASUNARI: Bimini water itself is radio-active, which produces greater elimination at a given temperature for a given time than other waters, leaving the skin soft and velvety as a babe's. That's why it's called the Velvet Bath. We also have red rays and blue rays.

MAXWELL: What are those?

REYNOLDS AS YASUNARI: Leucodescent lamp manipulations.

MAXWELL: Is it safe?

REYNOLDS AS YASUNARI: *(Seating* MAXWELL*)* Its rays are anodyne, antiseptic, antiphlogistic, and absolutely safe.

MAXWELL: Have you tried it yourself?

REYNOLDS AS YASUNARI: I'm not permitted, sir. Please sit perfectly still for greatest effect.

(A blue light beams on MAXWELL. REYNOLDS *removes the jacket and sits next to* MAXWELL.*)*

MAXWELL: After this treatment we will enter the plunge. You'll find it quite refreshing. *(After a moment)* I believe Mr Yasunari has gone.

(REYNOLDS *looks around for* YASUNARI.*)*

REYNOLDS: My self-study has indeed been revealing.

MAXWELL: About your childhood? What have you discovered?

REYNOLDS: Every young boy desires a mentor, an adult male who initiates him into manhood. Surely you had someone to instruct you.

MAXWELL: As I mentioned, one of our boarders, Professor Frank Moody, was inspirational to me.

REYNOLDS: What was he professor of?

MAXWELL: Professor was mostly a nickname. A British typewriter supply salesman who dreamed of higher things.

REYNOLDS: For himself and for you.

MAXWELL: Although I possessed an innate aesthetic sense, there was no art education available to the son of a cabinetmaker in Santa Ana in those days.

REYNOLDS: Professor Moody did you a great service.

(REYNOLDS *turns into* MOODY.)

MAXWELL: I was most grateful for the attention. My father's long hours in the shop left little time for his only child.

(Lighting turns red.)

REYNOLDS AS MOODY: *(English accent)* One must experience art in all dimensions, Everett. A successful painting explodes beyond width and height to invite us into its depth. The most evocative sculpture has sensual movement, transcending three-dimensionality to embrace—

(MAXWELL *becomes a pubescent version of himself,* YOUNG MAXWELL.)

YOUNG MAXWELL: Time, the fourth dimension!

REYNOLDS AS MOODY: That's exactly right, Everett! Brilliant! What tableaux have you to show me?

(YOUNG MAXWELL *poses.)*

REYNOLDS AS MOODY: *David!* By…?

YOUNG MAXWELL: Michelangelo! *(Poses)*

REYNOLDS AS MOODY: *Discobolus!* Artist?

YOUNG MAXWELL: Myron of Eleutherae! *(Poses)*

REYNOLDS AS MOODY: *Shiva as Lord of the Dance!* Sculptor?

YOUNG MAXWELL: Unknown!

REYNOLDS AS MOODY: You can do better than that.

YOUNG MAXWELL: Anonymous Indian! Chola period! Tamil Nadu!

REYNOLDS AS MOODY: You haven't got it quite. *(Adjusts* YOUNG MAXWELL*'s pose)* A little more…yes…hold still. I know it's difficult to strike a balance, but you're destroying and creating the universe simultaneously—one can't expect that to be easy.

YOUNG MAXWELL: Let's do paintings, Professor!

REYNOLDS AS MOODY: Very well.

YOUNG MAXWELL: Give me a title. Anything!

REYNOLDS AS MOODY: *The Scream.*

(YOUNG MAXWELL *poses.)*

REYNOLDS AS MOODY: Botticelli's *Birth of Venus.*

(YOUNG MAXWELL *poses)*

REYNOLDS AS MOODY: Da Vinci's *Last Supper.*

(YOUNG MAXWELL *does a quick sequence of all 13 figures from left to right.)*

REYNOLDS AS MOODY: Manet's *Odalisque*!

(YOUNG MAXWELL *reclines in the sexy pose of the painting.* REYNOLDS AS MOODY *studies him a moment.)*

REYNOLDS AS MOODY: Impressive. You've earned your next art lesson.

YOUNG MAXWELL: What is it?

REYNOLDS AS MOODY: Some very special images.

YOUNG MAXWELL: Which artist?

REYNOLDS AS MOODY: As we've discussed, some artists wish to remain anonymous.

(REYNOLDS AS MOODY *produces the notebook.* YOUNG MAXWELL *registers some concern about how* REYNOLDS *got it back.)*

YOUNG MAXWELL: What's that?

REYNOLDS AS MOODY: A rare portfolio.

YOUNG MAXWELL: Are they prints?

REYNOLDS AS MOODY: Photographs.

YOUNG MAXWELL: Photography isn't art!

REYNOLDS AS MOODY: These photographs are.

(REYNOLDS AS MOODY *shows* YOUNG MAXWELL *a page of the notebook.* YOUNG MAXWELL *reacts,* REYNOLDS AS MOODY *noting the reaction.* REYNOLDS AS MOODY *turns the pages.* YOUNG MAXWELL *reacts slightly differently. Several pages, with increasing reactions from* YOUNG MAXWELL. *For one he may turn his head sideways for a better look, for another, he may try take the notebook to reorient it. But* REYNOLDS AS MOODY *won't let go.)*

REYNOLDS AS MOODY: What do you think?

YOUNG MAXWELL: I've never seen those poses before.

REYNOLDS AS MOODY: But you find them interesting?

YOUNG MAXWELL: That one hurts. Look at his face.

REYNOLDS AS MOODY: That's passion.

YOUNG MAXWELL: Like a crucifixion?

REYNOLDS AS MOODY: It hurts in a nice way. When you're older, you'll understand.

YOUNG MAXWELL: I think I understand now.

REYNOLDS AS MOODY: How old are you, Everett?

YOUNG MAXWELL: Old! Almost thirteen!

REYNOLDS AS MOODY: Only adults understand.

YOUNG MAXWELL: I'm precocious. You said so.

REYNOLDS AS MOODY: That's true. But it's not good to grow up too fast. Once you do, you can never go back.

YOUNG MAXWELL: In the Jewish religion you become an adult at thirteen.

REYNOLDS AS MOODY: But you're not even the smallest part Jewish, Everett. *(Pause)* Are you?

*(*YOUNG MAXWELL *looks very uncomfortable then turns suddenly back into* MAXWELL.*)*

MAXWELL: Art! We only talked about art!

*(*REYNOLDS *turns back into himself. The red light goes off and normal lighting returns.)*

MAXWELL: I was being educated!

REYNOLDS: I thought I recognized the Socratic method.

MAXWELL: I'm not like you. I have no...destructive urge!

REYNOLDS: Oh, no. You're full of life. In fact, you remind me very much of Victor.

MAXWELL: Victor Lamar? That Bohemian lad?

REYNOLDS: So anxious to grow up. It got him into trouble, too.

MAXWELL: Trouble? What kind of trouble?

REYNOLDS: He brought it on himself.

*(*REYNOLDS *dons the white jacket and becomes* YASUNARI.*)*

MAXWELL: Fourteen year-olds are just…exploring. They want to see how far they can go, what they can get away with—they're boys—!

REYNOLDS AS YASUNARI: Mr Maxwell, are you ready for the plunge?

MAXWELL: *(Going with* YASUNARI*)* Oh! Mr Yasunari! Yes, I believe we've had quite enough treatments for one evening.

REYNOLDS AS YASUNARI: A refreshing Velvet Bath would be just the thing. I am told it's soothing and relaxing.

*(*MAXWELL *enters the pool.)*

MAXWELL: Edward, join me! This plunge is the essence of the famous Bimini Baths, the reason the resort was built.

*(*REYNOLDS *takes off the jacket and becomes himself.)*

MAXWELL: The mineral water six degrees above body temperature, the continual flow of freshness—think of it as a baptism—

REYNOLDS: And clean?

MAXWELL: What do you mean?

REYNOLDS: Exclusive?

MAXWELL: Mr Yasunari has never been in the water, so I assume.

*(*REYNOLDS *enters the pool.)*

REYNOLDS: Ahhh!

MAXWELL: Nothing like this in Oklahoma, I'll wager! What luxury!

REYNOLDS: I feel thirty years younger already.

MAXWELL: I'm delighted you're feeling better. No more talk of annihilation.

REYNOLDS: Are you enjoying the plunge, Victor?

MAXWELL: What?

REYNOLDS: I'm so glad you brought me here. But you shouldn't have lied about your age to get in.

MAXWELL: What are you talking about? Bimini Baths admits all ages.

REYNOLDS: I would have been happy to pay adult admission for you. It's only ten cents more.

*(*MAXWELL *resists, but slowly turns into* VICTOR LAMAR, *age 13. He develops a more youthful voice and a Bohemian accent.)*

MAXWELL: I was full price!

REYNOLDS: Victor, you're far too concerned with economics.

MAXWELL: Quit calling me Victor!

REYNOLDS: I'll call you what I wish. I paid good money.

MAXWELL AS VICTOR: You can't treat me like some little kid. *(He doesn't appear to be an especially expert swimmer.)*

REYNOLDS: That's true, Victor. You're a young man who understands. You know how the world works. You know the value of your time. You know the value of fun.

MAXWELL AS VICTOR: Nothing wrong with getting three or four dollars to have a good time.

REYNOLDS: Please don't talk about money.

MAXWELL AS VICTOR: You brung it up.

REYNOLDS: There are people all around.

MAXWELL AS VICTOR: They're swimming—ain't paying us no mind.

REYNOLDS: That's true. But it doesn't hurt to be careful.

MAXWELL AS VICTOR: I look after myself.

REYNOLDS: And it doesn't pay to be reckless.

MAXWELL AS VICTOR: I ain't reckless! I know what I can do.

REYNOLDS: Can you actually swim, Victor?

MAXWELL AS VICTOR: You bet!

REYNOLDS: You're dog-paddling. Let me teach you real skills.

MAXWELL AS VICTOR: I can swim!

REYNOLDS: *(Demonstrating)* This is Australian crawl.

MAXWELL AS VICTOR: Yeah, I know.

REYNOLDS: *(Stroking)* This is the backstroke.

MAXWELL AS VICTOR: *(Awkwardly imitating)* I know! I'm not a kid!

REYNOLDS: *(Stroking)* The breaststroke.

MAXWELL AS VICTOR: *(Awkwardly imitating)* I know that one, too!

REYNOLDS: *(Stroking)* Butterfly.

MAXWELL AS VICTOR: This ain't the first time I been here!

REYNOLDS: *(Stroking)* East Indian stroke.

MAXWELL AS VICTOR: I know 'em all!

REYNOLDS: Someone's got to watch you like a hawk or you'll sink!

MAXWELL AS VICTOR: I can breaststroke! I can crawl!

REYNOLDS: Maybe we should start you out in one of the swimming harnesses till you learn some technique.

MAXWELL AS VICTOR: Harnesses are for girls! I got technique! *(He hauls himself out of the pool.)* I can freestyle! I can backstroke! Frontstroke! Sidestroke!

REYNOLDS: Victor, be careful!

MAXWELL AS VICTOR: Butterfly, dragonfly, shoo-fly!

REYNOLDS: The edge is slick!

MAXWELL AS VICTOR: I can dive, too! You think I can't? *(He starts climbing high above* REYNOLDS.*)*

REYNOLDS: You've never dived before in your life!

MAXWELL AS VICTOR: I been practicing! You think I only come here with you?

REYNOLDS: Lifeguard, watch him!

MAXWELL AS VICTOR: I got lots of friends like you! Grown up chums who treat me right, better than you!

REYNOLDS: He has no idea what he's doing!

MAXWELL AS VICTOR: I know what I'm doing! I can swan dive, cannonball—

REYNOLDS: Lifeguard! Attendant! Do you hear me?

MAXWELL AS VICTOR: I can do a plain dive, a fancy dive—

MAXWELL AS VICTOR: —A running dive— *(Pauses at the top of the dive platform)* —A high dive—

REYNOLDS: Victor, come down! That's way too high for your first time.

MAXWELL AS VICTOR: *(Scared)* Ain't too high for me!

REYNOLDS: Someone get him down!

MAXWELL AS VICTOR: *(Bravado)* Ain't my first time!

REYNOLDS: Where's the manager? Who has charge of safety?

MAXWELL AS VICTOR: I can dive!

*(*MAXWELL AS VICTOR *jumps from the high dive. It's sad, happy, strange and hurts. He falls slowly as* REYNOLDS *speaks.)*

REYNOLDS: I tried to stop him, but he threw himself off the high platform as if casting himself into hell. He lost his balance before he left the board, twisted, gasped, crushed his forehead on the corner of the platform and careered sideways instead of straight into the plunge. His trajectory seemed physically impossible, the angle so— torturous—almost as if he was swept aside by the vengeful hand of God. At the first crack, everyone in the water snapped their heads toward the dive, staring, frozen, as Victor slowly, slowly plummeted, like a humorously awkward diving bird, a cormorant, a water turkey, the crimson slice above his eye visible to all. No one screamed, no one took a breath. Even the gush of the hot spring water seemed to pause as Victor plunged like Icarus. Only when his head cracked a second time—against the travertine coping on the edge of the pool—was there a collective groan, as if every one of us suffered his hurt. Only then did a lifeguard appear. Only then did a cadre of colored attendants fish him from the tank and apply the usual restoratives, to no avail. They refused to abandon the effort long after all hope was gone, and their severe methods left the body almost unrecognizable as the beautiful lad so passionate and full of life only minutes before.

(Upon landing, MAXWELL AS VICTOR *turns back into* MAXWELL.*)*

MAXWELL: I remember! Now I remember!

REYNOLDS: What?

MAXWELL: This really happened!

REYNOLDS: Of course it did, I just told you. Terrible.

MAXWELL: Five years ago, ten years ago—

REYNOLDS: It was 1908.

MAXWELL: Almost a decade ago! But you made it sound like it just occurred.

REYNOLDS: For me it will always be a fresh tragedy.

MAXWELL: But that's not how it happened.

REYNOLDS: How would you know?

MAXWELL: It made the papers! *(Reads from a clipping)* "The death of young Victor Lamar who was drowned at Bimini Baths on October 28, is recalled by an action—"

REYNOLDS: You saved clippings?	MAXWELL: "—Filed in the Superior Court yesterday—"
REYNOLDS: And you carry them around with you? Why?	MAXWELL: "—By Vaclav Lamar of number 402 Centennial Street, who asks from the Bimini Water Company twenty thousand dollars."
REYNOLDS: Even I didn't keep the clippings and I was there!	MAXWELL: "The petition recites that the defendant was derelict in its duty in the conduct of the bathing place—"
REYNOLDS: What do you expect from the *Los Angeles Times*? Made it sensational when it was intimately tragic.	MAXWELL: "—In not employing suitable guards and proper appliances to keep persons from death by drowning."

*(*MAXWELL *suddenly turns into* VICTOR.*)*

MAXWELL AS VICTOR: Father, I been meaning to ask you—

REYNOLDS: What are you doing?

MAXWELL AS VICTOR: This ain't the first time you done this.

REYNOLDS: Who are you now?

MAXWELL AS VICTOR: Don't act like you forgot your precious little Victor already.

REYNOLDS: You can't just—become—!

MAXWELL AS VICTOR: I do what I want! I'm old enough!

REYNOLDS: You're a grown man.

MAXWELL AS VICTOR: Not everybody agrees with that. Some might say I'm unlawful.

REYNOLDS: Don't say that, Victor. Let's not talk—let's swim!

MAXWELL AS VICTOR: I wanna talk before any swimming. Four dollars ain't much.

REYNOLDS: More than you've ever seen!

MAXWELL AS VICTOR: My company's worth more than that. *Ja Vam stojim za dobry penize!* [I'm worth good money!]

REYNOLDS: I've been most generous!

MAXWELL AS VICTOR: And keeping my mouth shut's worth more still.

REYNOLDS: Victor. What do you know of such things?

MAXWELL AS VICTOR: Like I said, I been here before. I ain't leaving this changing room till you give me sufficient.

REYNOLDS: Sufficient? Do you even know what that means? You barely know English!

MAXWELL AS VICTOR: Sufficient to shut my mouth.

REYNOLDS: *(Going to him)* Victor, who put these ideas in your head? Your chums? Who've you told about me?

MAXWELL AS VICTOR: Nobody yet! Nor will I if I get sufficient!

REYNOLDS: Absolutely, Victor. I understand your position. I've taken advantage of your youth, your naiveté, your recent arrival in this country. I'll most certainly give you—

(REYNOLDS *quickly overpowers* MAXWELL AS VICTOR *and slams his head against a wall with an audible crack.)*

REYNOLDS: Sufficient.

(REYNOLDS *throws* MAXWELL AS VICTOR *into the pool. Sound of a splash.* MAXWELL *floats as if unconscious.)*

MAXWELL: *(Quoting as if somnambulant)* "An application for a criminal complaint has been made, and it is the belief of the Lamar family and others that the boy met with foul play."

REYNOLDS: That's not what happened.

MAXWELL: "It is also alleged that E V Reynolds, a moral degenerate, was allowed to attack Lamar in one of the bathrooms—"

REYNOLDS: He struck his head on the diving board, the coping—

MAXWELL: "—And that when the two were in the water Reynolds again attacked his companion, striking him on the head and stunning him.

REYNOLDS: I was the only witness, it wasn't a busy day—the baths deserted—

MAXWELL: "Several surgeons examined the body and agreed that the boy had been the victim of horrible mistreatment."

REYNOLDS: I couldn't find staff—no competent attendants—just slow dark men—

MAXWELL: "A secret autopsy was held under direction of the District Attorney's office, and an early arrest is anticipated as a result of the finding."

REYNOLDS: I thought you understood.

(MAXWELL *comes out of the water.)*

MAXWELL: I understand. I was there.

REYNOLDS: Where?

*(*MAXWELL *starts putting on clothes, not the tuxedo he wore previously, but plain cotton in black-and-white stripes.)*

MAXWELL: The changing room of Bimini Baths on the morning of October 28, 1908. The next cubicle.

REYNOLDS: Why would you listen to a private conversation?

MAXWELL: I recognized one of the voices.

REYNOLDS: You've only just met me.

MAXWELL: Victor. I knew Victor.

REYNOLDS: You knew him. You've been far from candid with me.

MAXWELL: His father Vaclav was friends with Max Wieczorek. The Bohemian community of Los Angeles sticks together.

REYNOLDS: You knew a boy like that in 1908.

MAXWELL: Really, I knew his father—

REYNOLDS: You knew boys like that ten years ago. You have history, a pattern of behavior!

MAXWELL: My behavior is nothing next to your—capital crime! You got away with murder. No arrest was ever made. Where did you go?

REYNOLDS: Las Vegas.

MAXWELL: Not back to Oklahoma?

REYNOLDS: I couldn't.

MAXWELL: So you hid out in Las Vegas.

REYNOLDS: I founded Saint Joan of Arc Catholic Church and stayed in Las Vegas until now.

MAXWELL: So you got away with it.

REYNOLDS: You failed to come forward. That makes you an accessory.

MAXWELL: Why do you think I've kept the clippings? Memorized them? Obsessed, suffered, sought atonement—I knew the boy! And I was afraid to step in, afraid my own—sins—would be known.

REYNOLDS: You admit to sins.

MAXWELL: All men sin!

REYNOLDS: But yours is the worst sin. The unforgiveable sin. It merits the death penalty. No one can sympathize with you. Even murderers hate your type. In prison, they have to separate you from the rest for your own protection, otherwise you don't live long—

MAXWELL: I never murdered anyone! I never feared a boy so much I smashed his brains out, drowned him—!

REYNOLDS: You damaged their minds, their souls, brutally, forever. I smashed his brains—how is that so very different?

*(*MAXWELL *suddenly turns into an enraged and sorrowful* VACLAV LAMAR, *the father of* VICTOR.*)*

MAXWELL AS VACLAV: *(Bohemian accent)* My boy! My Victor!

REYNOLDS: No, no—don't—

MAXWELL AS VACLAV: He was good boy!

REYNOLDS: Mr Lamar, it was an accident—

MAXWELL AS VACLAV: Good Catholic boy and you corrupt him!

REYNOLDS: Your boy was not so innocent!

MAXWELL AS VACLAV: You are man of God, but what is God if you are this?

REYNOLDS: He was corrupt when I met him!

MAXWELL AS VACLAV: We give our children to church to be safe, to be holy, and you betray like Judas!

REYNOLDS: He was a degenerate old man in the body of a boy!

MAXWELL AS VACLAV: You kill—you crucify—like Jews!

REYNOLDS: I did none of that!

MAXWELL AS VACLAV: You baptize him in filth! Give him piss for wine and shit for holy body of Christ!

REYNOLDS: I loved him! As any pastor loves his flock!

MAXWELL AS VACLAV: That is your sacred communion of death!

MAXWELL AS VACLAV: You no love him. His family love him! *Byl to muj kluk a ted je pryc! Ukradeny!* [He was my boy and now gone! Stolen!] Violated! You no love—you destroy!

*(*MAXWELL *is now fully dressed in prison garb. Lighting changes to reveal they are in a cramped prison cell with a small prison bed.)*

REYNOLDS: That conversation never happened.

MAXWELL: Because you fled to the desert.

REYNOLDS: How arrogant to imagine you know how he felt.

MAXWELL: I didn't. Until now.

REYNOLDS: The art of empathy.

MAXWELL: In conversation with a monster.

REYNOLDS: Your empathy extends to me. To a monster.

*(*MAXWELL *is silent.)*

REYNOLDS: Confess. I'll never rest until you do.

MAXWELL: I may or may not have done wrong. But you committed murder. And you escaped.

REYNOLDS: I have not. It's always with me.

MAXWELL: You deserve prison.

REYNOLDS: But you're the one got caught.

MAXWELL: Haven't you been caught? We're both in San Quentin.

REYNOLDS: I'm your spiritual counselor.

MAXWELL: The prison chaplain? Dressed like that?

REYNOLDS: You're seeing what you wish to see. Perhaps you're the one going mad. Didn't your attorney attempt to have you declared insane to reduce your sentence?

MAXWELL: He was…not successful.

REYNOLDS: But now you're imagining the prison chaplain shirtless. *(He retrieves his shirt and Roman collar, puts it on.)* Seeing people who aren't there.

MAXWELL: You're not the chaplain. You're a prisoner. You've finally been caught!

REYNOLDS: But aren't you supposed to be in solitary confinement—?

MAXWELL: Yes—

REYNOLDS: For your own safety, according to regulations for all men convicted of statutory crimes?

MAXWELL: I haven't been convicted! I haven't confessed!

REYNOLDS: Which is why your sentence—at the moment—is indefinite. If you'd actually confess, your attorney could get you paroled.

MAXWELL: I'll file a complaint. Your presence here is a violation.

REYNOLDS: There's only one bed.

MAXWELL: The warden is responsible for prisoner safety.

REYNOLDS: And I've a history of violence.

MAXWELL: I'm not intimidated.

REYNOLDS: You're on suicide watch.

*(*MAXWELL *is silent)*

REYNOLDS: You're not like the other boys. You're special. Isn't that what you told Zenobio Remedios?

MAXWELL: He is special! Not a boy whore like your Victor! Zeno has aptitude!

REYNOLDS: A bright thirteen year-old.

MAXWELL: He's sixteen!

REYNOLDS: Now. In 1918. But on December 6, 1915 when you took him for a hike in the tall grass of the Arroyo Seco, he was only thirteen. The same age you were when Professor Frank Moody inculcated you in art. *(He puts on a white jacket.)*

MAXWELL: I was twelve, actually.

REYNOLDS: Sorry, I forgot. Twelve!

MAXWELL: You're making him sound nefarious! Frank did me no harm!

REYNOLDS: He opened up the world for you.

MAXWELL: He cared for me.

REYNOLDS: He brought you into adulthood. A rite of passage.

MAXWELL: As I care for Zeno.

REYNOLDS: Would Zeno say that?

MAXWELL: Yes! He cares for me, too!

REYNOLDS: You can't even see him. You're imagining the boy you want. Did he want what happened in the tunnel of weeds? *(He takes out the notebook and pen.)*

MAXWELL: Nothing happened! But if it had, he would have welcomed it, yes.

REYNOLDS: *(Makes a note)* I see.

MAXWELL: How'd you get that back?

REYNOLDS: My sermon notes?

MAXWELL: My notebook. You gave it to me but now you have it again.

REYNOLDS: You're remembering incorrectly. Interesting. *(Makes a note)*

MAXWELL: You're not a priest at all, are you?

REYNOLDS: No.

MAXWELL: Nor a prisoner.

REYNOLDS: Metaphorically, I suppose.

MAXWELL: You're an alienist.

REYNOLDS: *(Makes a note)* Hmmm.

MAXWELL: That's why you know so much about pedophilia, hebephilia, ephebophilia—anal puckering—criminal penises—!

REYNOLDS: Go on.

MAXWELL: You're writing down everything I say!

REYNOLDS: I'm much more interested in what you write down.

MAXWELL: Evidence!

REYNOLDS: I'm trying to help you.

MAXWELL: To trap me!

REYNOLDS: You've trapped yourself. I can get you out. You're right. I am a psychiatrist, hired by the Museum to observe you.

MAXWELL: Why?

REYNOLDS: According to your doctor you've been in a delicate psychological state for quite some time.

MAXWELL: Since these false accusations!

REYNOLDS: Since you were thirteen. Perhaps all your life.

MAXWELL: Why would the Museum hire an alienist?

REYNOLDS: They care for you. And they want me to convince you to sign this. *(Proffers the notebook)*

MAXWELL: A confession?

REYNOLDS: It's your own words.

MAXWELL: You've put them in my mouth!

REYNOLDS: I've elicited them. There's a legal difference. If you sign a confession, your sentence will become probation and you'll be released. You've already served a year in San Quentin.

Isn't that enough atonement for you?

MAXWELL: I've nothing to atone for!

REYNOLDS: Not according to this letter from the Museum's President to the Clerk of the State Board of Prisons.

*(*REYNOLDS *hands a letter to* MAXWELL *then becomes* BOWEN.*)*

REYNOLDS AS BOWEN: I am very glad indeed to see that some effort is being made to help Mr Everett C. Maxwell. He was employed in the Los Angeles County Museum of History, Science and Art from November 25th, 1913 to April 1st, 1916, as Curator of Art, the most important branch in our institution. He came to us highly recommended by leading citizens who stood for the higher things in this community and during the period of his employment, although brought in contact with thousands of people weekly, there was not a word against his character as a useful citizen and a gentleman.

MAXWELL: Bowen supports me!

REYNOLDS AS BOWEN: By one act all this was destroyed, and the lives of his father and mother practically wrecked. Personally, I believe that he has been severely punished already, and if his conduct has been worthy during the time he has spent at San Quentin I sincerely trust that the State Board of Prison Directors or the Board of Parole will do all they can to give this boy a chance to commence over. Yours very truly, William Bowen, President.

MAXWELL: *(Devastated)* He wrote that?

REYNOLDS: Mistaken identity, my ass.

MAXWELL: Even Bowen thinks I did it?

REYNOLDS: Nothing exists until written. *(Proffers notebook)* Write it, sign it, and you shall go free. This is why I'm here.

MAXWELL: I've told this story a thousand times! To the marshal, to Zeno's *abuelo*—

REYNOLDS: This time, tell the truth.

MAXWELL: —To the attorneys, to the judge—

REYNOLDS: In Zeno's words.

MAXWELL: To the parole board—

*(*REYNOLDS *becomes* MAXWELL. *It's cruelly accurate.)*

REYNOLDS AS MAXWELL: He saw me smile and turned modestly away, pretending to examine a western tiger swallowtail pausing on a stem of California brome.

MAXWELL: Those are my words, but—

REYNOLDS AS MAXWELL: I reassured him with a touch that none could see—

MAXWELL: How could I know Zeno's words?

REYNOLDS AS MAXWELL: We were alone. He smiled, his face so open, his eyes so kind.

MAXWELL: How Zeno felt? Arrogant to imagine I would know.

REYNOLDS AS MAXWELL: I could see—

MAXWELL: I can't be—!

REYNOLDS AS MAXWELL: I could see—

*(*MAXWELL *starts turning into* ZENO.*)*

MAXWELL: You can't force me to—!

REYNOLDS: I could see that the struggle would be beautiful.

*(*REYNOLDS *puts* MAXWELL *in the Saint Sebastian pose.)*

MAXWELL AS ZENO: Saint Sebastian!

REYNOLDS AS MAXWELL: By Guido Reni! Zeno, you're a very smart lad. But the tableau isn't quite complete.

MAXWELL AS ZENO: What's missing, Mr Maxwell?

*(*REYNOLDS AS MAXWELL *tears a strip from the prison bedsheet, turns it into binding.)*

REYNOLDS AS MAXWELL: Saint Sebastian was tied to a tree by the Roman soldiers.

MAXWELL AS ZENO: Oh.

REYNOLDS AS MAXWELL: Shall we bind you for authenticity?

MAXWELL AS ZENO: I guess so.

REYNOLDS AS MAXWELL: *(Tying* MAXWELL*'s hands)* It adds tension to the composition.

MAXWELL AS ZENO: Ow.

REYNOLDS AS MAXWELL: Does it hurt?

MAXWELL AS ZENO: A little.

REYNOLDS AS MAXWELL: That's passion. Happy, sad—

MAXWELL AS ZENO: Strange—

REYNOLDS AS MAXWELL: And it hurts a little.

*(*REYNOLDS *starts unbuttoning* MAXWELL*'s prison garb, pulling it down so* MAXWELL *is naked from the waist up. At the same time,* REYNOLDS *becomes* FRANK MOODY.*)*

REYNOLDS AS MOODY: One must experience art in all dimensions, Everett. A successful painting explodes beyond width and height to invite us into its depth. *(Adjusts* MAXWELL*'s pose)* A little more…yes…hold still. I know it's difficult to strike a balance, but you're destroying and creating the universe simultaneously—one can't expect that to be easy.

(Without moving, MAXWELL *becomes* YOUNG MAXWELL. REYNOLDS AS MOODY *produces a camera.)*

REYNOLDS AS MOODY: Impressive. You've earned your next art lesson.

YOUNG MAXWELL: What is it, Frank?

REYNOLDS AS MOODY: You'll let me take your photograph in your birthday suit, won't you, Everett?

YOUNG MAXWELL: Like those you showed me?

REYNOLDS AS MOODY: Yes, like those artists who wish to remain anonymous. *(He takes some photographs.)*

YOUNG MAXWELL: Then can we visit the Ostrich Farm?

REYNOLDS AS MOODY: Yes. Hold still and I'll give you a cigarette. And pay you five cents.

*(*MAXWELL *turns into* VICTOR.*)*

MAXWELL AS VICTOR: Father, I been meaning to ask you—this ain't the first time you been to Bimini with a boy.

(REYNOLDS *turns back into himself.)*

REYNOLDS: Don't say that, Victor. Let's not talk—let's swim!

MAXWELL AS VICTOR: I wanna talk before any swimming. Four dollars ain't much.

REYNOLDS: More than you've ever seen!

MAXWELL AS VICTOR: My company's worth more than that. *Ja Vam stojim za dobry penize!* [I'm worth good money!]

REYNOLDS: I've been most generous! *(He puts down the camera and stands close behind* MAXWELL.*)*

MAXWELL AS VICTOR: And keeping my mouth shut's worth more still.

REYNOLDS: Victor. What do you know of such things? Who put these ideas in your head? Your chums? Who've you told about me?

MAXWELL AS VICTOR: Nobody yet! Nor will I if I get sufficient!

REYNOLDS: Absolutely, Victor. I understand your position. I've taken advantage of your youth, your naivete, your recent arrival in this country. I'll most certainly give you—

(REYNOLDS *thrusts into* MAXWELL. *There is the sound of a crack like the cracking of* VICTOR*'s skull.)*

(MAXWELL *gasps.)*

REYNOLDS: Sufficient.

(MAXWELL *turns back into* YOUNG MAXWELL.*)*

YOUNG MAXWELL: *(In pain)* Professor Moody, I think—!

*(*REYNOLDS *turns back into* FRANK MOODY, *continues thrusting.)*

REYNOLDS AS MOODY: Shhh! Be quiet, Everett.

YOUNG MAXWELL: But, Professor—!

REYNOLDS AS MOODY: Shhh!

YOUNG MAXWELL: I don't understand!

REYNOLDS AS MOODY: You understand, Everett.

YOUNG MAXWELL: I do?

REYNOLDS AS MOODY: You understand perfectly. You don't need to say a word.

YOUNG MAXWELL: Not a word?

REYNOLDS AS MOODY: Be silent.

YOUNG MAXWELL: Silent?

REYNOLDS AS MOODY: Silent as a work of art. Silent as stone!

*(*REYNOLDS *turns into* MAXWELL, *continues thrusting.)*

REYNOLDS AS MAXWELL: What artist makes you feel the most, Zeno?

*(*MAXWELL *turns back into* ZENO.*)*

MAXWELL AS ZENO: *(In pain)* What…artist?

REYNOLDS AS MAXWELL: You just told me.

MAXWELL AS ZENO: Guido Reni?

REYNOLDS AS MAXWELL: Yes! You are so smart, Zeno. Smarter than the other boys.

MAXWELL AS ZENO: I am?

REYNOLDS AS MAXWELL: Smarter and special. You know what art is about.

MAXWELL AS ZENO: Feeling?

REYNOLDS AS MAXWELL: Yes! The purpose of art is empathy! We want to feel!

MAXWELL AS ZENO: I feel—

REYNOLDS AS MAXWELL: You feel nice.

MAXWELL AS ZENO: No, I feel—

*(*REYNOLDS AS MAXWELL *is approaching orgasm.)*

REYNOLDS AS MAXWELL: Special.

MAXWELL AS ZENO: No, Mr Maxwell—*por favor—*

REYNOLDS AS MAXWELL: What do you feel, Zeno?

MAXWELL AS ZENO: *Me duele! Siento dolor!* [It hurts! I feel pain!]

REYNOLDS AS MAXWELL: It's what you want, Zeno! To feel! *Sentir!*

MAXWELL AS ZENO: *No lo quiero!* [I don't want it!]

REYNOLDS AS MAXWELL: Art is feeling! Art is pain!

MAXWELL AS ZENO: *Por favor, Señor Maxwell!*

*(*REYNOLDS *turns back into himself.)*

REYNOLDS: *Esto es lo que significa—* [This is what it means—]

MAXWELL AS ZENO: *¡Pare! ¡Por favor pare!* [Stop! Please stop!]

*(*REYNOLDS *climaxes.)*

REYNOLDS: *—Ser un hombre!* [To be a man!]

(Once again the sound of the cracking of a skull. MAXWELL AS ZENO *falls down crying.)*

MAXWELL AS ZENO: *Eso no es lo que quería! No entiendia! Es lo que usted quería! No lo que yo quiera!* [That's not what I wanted!

REYNOLDS: *(Reads a criminal complaint)* Everett C Maxwell did feloniously commit a lewd and lascivious act upon

I didn't understand! It's what you wanted! I didn't want it!]

and with the body of Zenobio Remedios, a child under the age of fourteen years with the intent of arousing, appealing and gratifying the lust and passion—

(As they speak, REYNOLDS *unties* MAXWELL*'s hands, and* MAXWELL *reaches back and touches himself. He looks at his hand, which is bloody.)*

MAXWELL AS ZENO: Señor Maxwell, does this mean you love me?

*(*MAXWELL *turns back into himself, his voice becoming more adult the longer he speaks. He desperately cleans the blood from his hand.)*

(The lighting becomes more focused.)

MAXWELL: *Pensé que sabía, pero aun no! Perdon! Me dije—* [I thought I knew, but I didn't! I'm sorry! I told myself] —it was all right! I didn't understand! Love!?

REYNOLDS: —And sexual desires of said Everett C Maxwell. *(He ties the fabric into a noose.)*

MAXWELL: I'm sorry, Zeno. I'm so sorry. *Lo siento.* I thought you were me at that age. You were my youth. I saw…myself in your smile. When I looked in your eyes. So kind.

*(*REYNOLDS *helps* MAXWELL *to his feet and up onto the bed. The lighting narrows into a shaft illuminating only* MAXWELL *standing on the bed.)*

MAXWELL: I didn't expect…a struggle. I hope I didn't hurt you…too much.

REYNOLDS: You invaded him like we did Mexico in 1916. Better if you'd drowned him in the Baths.

MAXWELL: I might as well have.

REYNOLDS: Then he couldn't have talked. You wouldn't be here.

MAXWELL: I'm not like you.

REYNOLDS: You're worse. You couldn't even see what you'd done.

MAXWELL: I see. *Ya veo.* I see very well.

*(*REYNOLDS *puts the noose around* MAXWELL*'s neck.)*

REYNOLDS: Then you're ready to atone. To be washed clean.

MAXWELL: You were never caught, were you, Reynolds? You fled Bimini and disappeared: Las Vegas, Oklahoma. Never imprisoned. Never in San Quentin. You're neither priest nor alienist nor any of the others you pretended to be. I'm alone in this room.

REYNOLDS: This cell.

MAXWELL: Solitary!

REYNOLDS: No way out. Except: *(Holds up the notebook)* I'm as real as this. Once you sign it. That's all I want.

*(*MAXWELL *reaches for the notebook, but* REYNOLDS *snatches it away and disappears in the surrounding darkness.)*

MAXWELL: Father? *(Pause)* Push me off! Knock over the bed! I can't do this by myself, Father! I don't want to be here! Help me! Only you can grant me absolution! This is my *noche oscura de alma.* I'm confessing! I want to atone, be clean! Please! I'll sign! Only knock it over! *(After a moment)* You're not here. You were never here. *(Pause. He struggles with the idea of kicking away from the bed, but can't bring himself to do it.)*

(After a moment, a pinspot comes up on a corner of the bed, illuminating the notebook and pen. MAXWELL *notices. He*

stares at it a little while, then takes the noose from his neck and steps down from the bed. He picks up the notebook and pen.)

MAXWELL: *(Reading)* I could see that the struggle would be beautiful.

(REYNOLDS AS ZENO *appears isolated in light.* MAXWELL *stares at him a moment.)*

MAXWELL: *(Makes a correction)* I could see that the struggle would be…brutal.

REYNOLDS AS ZENO: Señor Maxwell, does this mean you love me?

(MAXWELL *stares at him again, then begins to write as the lights slowly fade.)*

END OF PLAY

www.ingramcontent.com/pod-product-compliance
Lightning Source LLC
Chambersburg PA
CBHW052223090426
42741CB00010B/2651
* 9 7 8 0 8 8 1 4 5 7 9 0 2 *